Young Jackie Robinson

Baseball Hero

A Troll First-Start Biography

by Edward Farrell
illustrated by Dennis Stuart

Troll Associates

Library of Congress Cataloging-in-Publication Data

Farrell, Edward, (date)
    Young Jackie Robinson, baseball hero / by Edward Farrell;
illustrated by Dennis Stuart.
        p.   cm.—(First-start biographies)
    Summary: A biography of the first black player in modern American
major league baseball, emphasizing the prejudice he had to overcome
by sheer courage.
    ISBN 0-8167-2536-5 (lib. bdg.)   ISBN 0-8167-2537-3 (pbk.)
    1. Robinson, Jackie, 1919-1972—Juvenile literature.   2. Baseball
players—United States—Biography—Juvenile literature.
[1. Robinson, Jackie, 1919-1972.   2. Baseball players.   3. Afro-
Americans—Biography.]   I. Stuart, Dennis, ill.   II. Title.
GV865.R6F37   1992
796.357'092—dc20
    [B]   91-26480

Jackie Robinson was the first black
man to play major-league baseball.
He opened the door to many other
black players.

3

Jackie was born in Georgia in 1919.
His parents were very poor. They
already had 4 children to feed.

Jackie was just a baby when his
mother took her children to California.
There wasn't much money to go
around, but there was a lot of love.

As Jackie grew up, he discovered there was a lot of conflict between blacks and whites. There was even a law that said blacks could not swim in the town pool with white children.

Jackie was angry at being treated unfairly. But he knew that fighting with his fists would only make things worse.

Instead, Jackie fought back by being
the best athlete he could.

In high school, Jackie was a star
athlete. No one played as hard as
he did.

When Jackie went to college, he was
one of the best athletes in the country.
Baseball, basketball, football, track—
Jackie starred in them all.

In 1941, America entered World War II. Jackie joined the army. But he hurt his ankle and couldn't fight. Instead he trained troops.

13

After the war ended, Jackie joined the
Kansas City Monarchs. They were a
Negro American Baseball League
team.

The Monarchs played great baseball.

But Negro League players were not paid
well. They traveled in "colored-only"
sections of buses and trains. They had
to stay in run-down hotels and could eat
only in certain restaurants.

In 1945, Jackie met a man named Branch Rickey. Rickey was the president of a major-league baseball team called the Brooklyn Dodgers. Rickey wanted to open up the major leagues to black players. But he knew his first black player would have to be strong enough not to fight with every person who insulted him.

Jackie Robinson was the man Rickey
was looking for. He asked Jackie to
join the Montreal Royals. They were
a minor-league team owned by the
Dodgers. Jackie said yes.

Jackie played hard for the Royals.
He helped them win a championship.
But not all people liked him.

In 1947, Jackie joined the Brooklyn Dodgers. He was in the major leagues!

But things did not get any easier for
Jackie. Two Dodgers asked to be
traded to a different team. They did
not want to play with a black man.

Other players tried to hurt Jackie
during games. And the fans often
shouted terrible things at him.

Jackie fought back the way he
always had. He played the best
baseball he could.

In his first year, Jackie stole more bases than any other player. The Dodgers won the National League championship. And Jackie was named Rookie of the Year.

In 1949, Jackie was voted the Most
Valuable Player. It was a great honor.

Jackie played with the Dodgers for 10 years. He helped them win 6 National League titles and one World Series.

In 1957, Jackie left baseball. In 1962, he became the first black man elected to the Baseball Hall of Fame.

As he got older, Jackie became very sick. But he still worked hard to help black people.

In 1972, Jackie Robinson died.
But he will always be remembered
as the man whose courage and
talent changed baseball—and
America—forever.